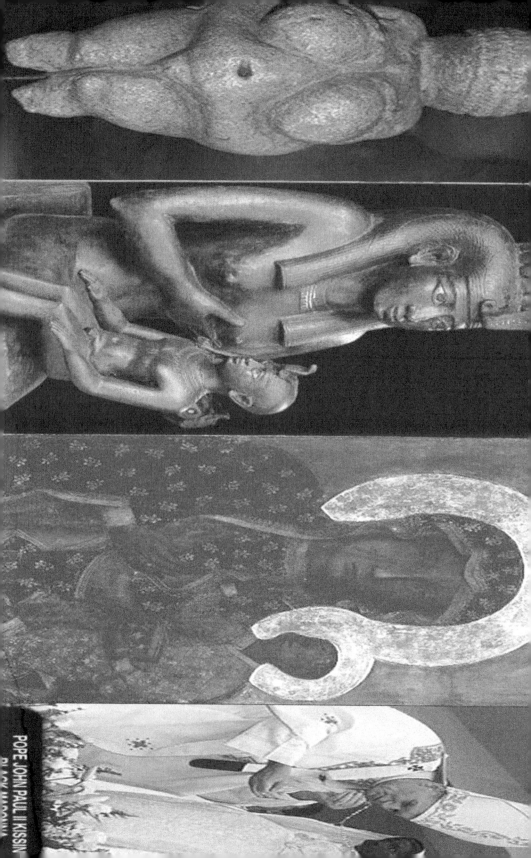

Fear of A Black Goddess

The Hidden History of the Divine Mother

by

Perry Kyles, Ph.D

African Diaspora Press

"An African worldview for an African world experience"

www.adponline.info

713-900-5062

THIS BOOK IS RESPECTFULLY
DEDICATED TO THE DIVINE MOTHERS
IN THE EARTHLY REALM.

Table of Contents

Introduction

A few years back the Houston Museum of Natural Science presented a display that was dedicated to the Virgin of Guadalupe, which is one of the most celebrated of the Madonna/Virgin Mary images in the world. Of the dozens of Madonna images in the exhibit and in the gift shop, each appeared with a European phenotype (physical features) or the skin tone was ambiguous. Soon after visiting the natural science museum, I had the opportunity to see firsthand the archived paintings at the Houston Museum of Fine Arts that were not on public display. I was surprised to see that there were several bold paintings of Black women whose images would fit perfectly among the images presented in this text. Furthermore, I saw a painting of the Virgin of Guadalupe that was unquestionably Black. How could the Black image of the Virgin of Guadalupe, and the other paintings of Black women, not be presented in the natural science museum exhibit less than a half-mile away or within any other Black art exhibit that has been presented at the fine arts museum?

The depths of the conspiracy became clearer when I became aware of the contrast between public and private images of the Madonna presented in Catholic Churches. Black Madonna images adorn the private chambers of Catholic bishops throughout the world. Why has the worshipping of this divine mother become hidden over recent centuries? *Fear of a Black Goddess* explains the origins of this worship and offers insight as to why some groups are threatened by public knowledge of an original Black Madonna. *Fear of a Black Goddess* makes it clear that the effort to hide these truths is part of a strategy to maintain control over the mind and body of the Black Woman in particular and the people of the world in general.

Many will be surprised to learn that contempt for women (a.k.a. misogyny) only became commonplace in Africa and the Americas in areas that engulfed by European expansion. Many of the generalizations that are made about human nature and the nature of the sexes are based on the European experience. In fact, European attitudes regarding Earth, sex relationships, and survival have come to be accepted as the norm. However the forefathers and foremothers of humanity would have glared disapprovingly at the sex wars that are a part of popular culture today. I have explained the emergence of this misogyny in my previous writings called *Beyond Maafa: Black History from Human Origins to Recent Times* and *The Book That Every Black Christian Should Read*. Those texts should be read along with this one.

This text will chart the progression of the divine mother concept through the *Ages*. Furthermore the text will explain why the divine mother/Black Madonna concept has largely been hidden or ignored. I predict that the Age of Aquarius will be most decisive for humanity. During this age either natural, spiritual, or human forces will force humanity to reestablish its original Southern Cradle culture or else humanity will spiral into the direction of non-existence. It is my hope that this small text will make some positive contribution to humanity's cultural and spiritual resurrection. This resurrection will not be possible within the milieu of misogyny and sex wars.

It is necessary to explain why I, a man, took it upon myself to write about the reality of feminine energy in the universe and among humanity. Obviously it is not possible for me to see the world through the lenses of a woman. However it would have been intellectually dishonest and spiritually decadent not to share these truths with the world as they became apparent to me in my archaeological and historical research. It is not my intention to argue for supremacy for any one sex. We are all subject to the laws of the universe. However, I recognize that one of the detrimental "–isms" in our world is misogyny, which manifests in various forms.[1]

I can only hope that those who find error with this work will have the heart and spirit to expand our collective knowledge regarding the topics that I have broached.

---

1. [1] mi·sog·y·ny   məˈsäjənē/   *noun* dislike of, contempt for, or ingrained prejudice against women.
   "she felt she was struggling against thinly disguised misogyny"

Chapter 1

The Divine Mother and Early Human Cultures

Contrary to the teachings of the Roman Catholic Church, "woman" did not emerge from the rib of Adam. To comprehend this fact, one simply has to explore the science of the mammal class to which humanity belongs. All mammals are impregnated by way of a sexual exchange between male and female members of the same species, or species that are relatively close from a genetic standpoint. Although woman "carry" the young, which is a feat that is worthy of great respect and adoration, each sex contributes the same number of chromosomes that provide the genetic coding for the embryo. In the case of humanity, each sex provides 23 chromosomes, with the last of the 23 pairs determining the sex of the child. That 23rd male contribution determines the sex of a child. If that particular chromosome is "X" the child will be a female; if it is "Y" then the child will be male.

In nature and as it relates to the progression of humanity, man's responsibility is not only to contribute DNA (deoxyribonucleic acid, which provides genetic coding), but to provide physical protection for the pregnant woman. The notion that it was man's original responsibility to provide food is misguided. Food provision was provided by both sexes and thus other women helped to provide food. To jump ahead just a bit, the notion of man being solely responsible for food acquisition comes from the development of European culture (a.k.a. the Northern Cradle) that came into existence as Europeans developed a diet rooted in flesh consumption in the colder regions of Europe. This was in contrast to the plant-based diet of the original humans. Europeans emerged hundreds of thousands of years after the original man and woman of Earth developed human culture in Africa. This reality is reflected in the fact that about 95% of Africa is lactose intolerant whereas lactose intolerance is relatively low in Europe.[1]

For a number of reasons that I will not address here, I speculate that the origins of humanity is about 1,000,000 years ago. We know for certain that humanity's existence goes back at least 350,000 years.[2] The analysis of artifacts such as the "Venus" statues renders the "Adam's rib" argument invalid even in a metaphorical sense. Early humanity did not conceive of woman as somehow coming out of man alone. Evidence makes a compelling case that "womanity" was celebrated and appreciated. One example is the Venus of Tan Tan, which was found in Morocco. This primitive statue is likely hundreds of thousands years old. The stone itself is dated to be between 300,000 – 500,000 years old. The stone appears to be modified to give the appearance of a voluptuous woman. As will be seen via this statue and other "Venus" statues, the voluptuousness of the woman appears to be a positive acknowledgement of femininity. While some scholars have argued that the

---

[1] This statistic is in reference to milk consumption from cows.
[2] See the following articles :
http://www.nature.com/nature/journal/v546/n7657/full/nature22336.html?foxtrotcallback=true#contrib-auth and
https://www.newscientist.com/article/dn23240-the-father-of-all-men-is-340000-years-old/

Venus of Tan Tan (Morocco)

formation of the stone was created by nature, the presence of manganese and iron on the statue upon its finding suggests that it was manipulated. Another reason why Tan Tan was doubted is because it pre-dated the previously accepted date for the origins of homo sapien sapiens (modern humans) of 200,000 years. However, as I mentioned previously, we now know that humanity was in the region of

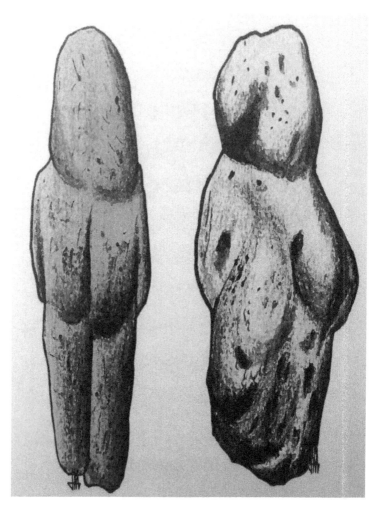

Venus of Berekhat Ram
(Israel/Syria)

contemporary Morocco as early as 350,000 years ago. The lack of rough edges compels me to say that it was manipulated by humans.

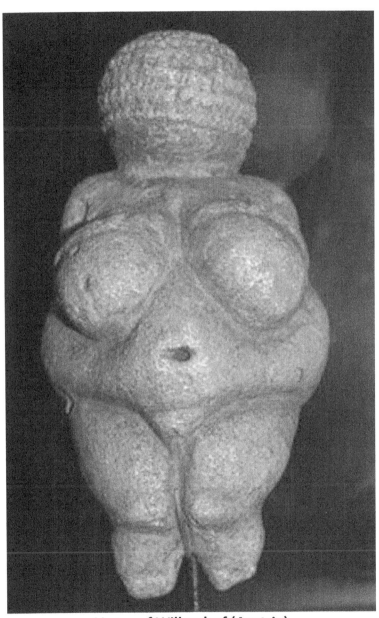

Venus of Willendorf (Austria)

Another of the Venus statues is the Venus of Berekhat Ram, which was found on the banks of Berekhat Ram (Lake Ram), in the Golan Heights between Syria and Isreal. The Venus of Berekhat Ram is also dated to be over 200,000 years old. This is also important because this particular Venus is very close to the location in Israel where the oldest human remains that have been found "outside of Africa".[3] There is no inherent reason why humans would have been in Morocco but not in the area known today as Israel.

It is important to mention that skillful crafts-making as well as mythological stories became more refined over the long march of human history. I surmise that this is the reason why each subsequent Venus appears to be more refined and apparent than previous carvings. One of the most refined of the Venuses presented in this text is the Venus of Willendorf that was found in Austria. She was dated to be over 25,000 years old. One of the reasons I surmise that Venus of Willendorf is a celebration of femininity and fertility is because the sex-related parts of her body are pronounced. Note that the breasts are full. Furthermore the vulva and the navel are exaggerated. Another reason why I conclude that the pre-historical Venus statues celebrate beauty or womanity is the presence of the hairstyle that we call today "Bantu knots". Why would the Bantu knots be across the face and not her head? To me, this strengthens the argument that the statue is symbolic and somewhat conceptual.

---

[3] I put "outside of Africa" in quotation marks because the contemporary boundaries as to where Africa begins and ends were artificially created in recent times.

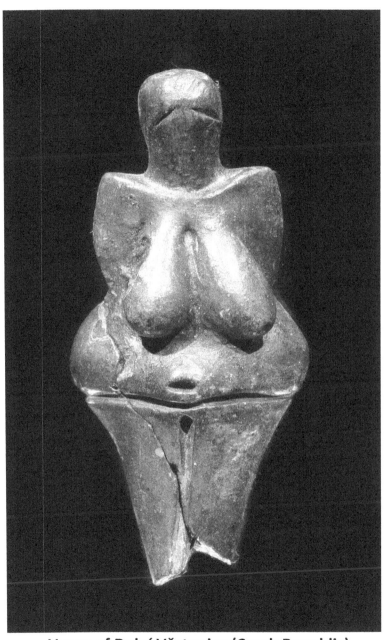

Venus of Dolní Věstonice (Czech Republic)

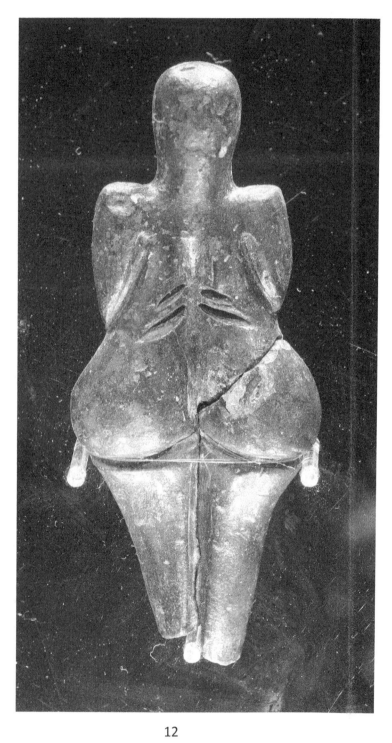

Lastly, I present here Venus of Dolní Věstonice. She was found in what is today the Czech Republic. She is reported to be about 28,000 years old. She was created with baked clay. As seen in the first image of her above, her breasts are full and her navel pronounced. Notice that both images present her with full hips, another reason to conclude that these Venus statues symbolize fertility in the human productive sense of in the agricultural sense.

The second image of the Venus of Dolní Věstonice reveals a full and rounded buttock. My theory, which is likely correct, is that the statue represents a celebration of womanity. The ages of the various Venus's suggest that the statues followed the pattern of human migration from the heartland of Africa to the other stretches of the world. Furthermore, the Venuses were ideally a Black female goddess. The latter two Venuses presented in this text were found to be between 25,000 and 30,000 years old and were found in the relatively low latitudes of Europe. I conclude that at this time the inhabitants of the region were still Africoid – meaning that they were Black with a Southern Cradle mindset. Even if there was "race-mixing", the Southern Cradle culture would have been present at that time. Additionally, we know that the buttocks of Dolní Věstonice reflect the physiological norm from within populations in the heartland of Africa. This is the physiological opposite of the Europeans that emerged from the northern stretches of Europe. The European populations that came from those northern stretches often suffered from rickets due to the lack of sunlight in the region. One of the consequences of rickets was a flattened buttocks.

The Venus statues reveal to us that as far back as 26,000 years ago, the divine mother was celebrated over a wide geographical spectrum of territory that had been colonized by humans. The next chapter will provide insight into the rise of misogyny over the course of the last 26,000 years.

Chapter 2

The Divine Mother Through The Ages

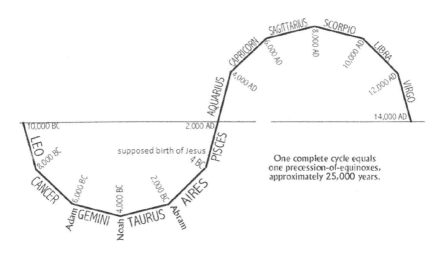

One complete cycle equals
one precession-of-equinoxes,
approximately 25,000 years.

The Current Processional Cycle

The most common method that is used to chart human history is the Gregorian calendar that was created in 1582 and credited to Pope Gregory XlII. However that calendar is insufficient to chart the broader periods of human history beyond the BC/AD era. Therefore I will use the periods of the precession of the Equinox to chart change in attitudes towards womanity.[1] A processional cycle is about 26,000 years and is broken down into twelve periods. Each period

---

[1] For a good introduction to the Precession of the Equinox, see Chapter 1 of Perry Kyles' *Beyond Maafa: Black History From Human Origins to Recent Times* (2017).

Ta-Urt

is commonly referred to as an *Age* and each is about 2,165 years. The current cycle began with the period of Leo, which began over 12,000 years ago. Currently we are in the latter years of the Piscean Age also known as the Age of Pisces. As I explained in the previous two sections of this book, European cultural norms have come to be accepted as "human nature". The ages of the Procession provides a convenient measuring stick to track how humanity's attitudes and beliefs towards the divine mother and feminine energy in general has changed over the course of this processional cycle.

We can approximate the attitude of humanity towards the divine mother during the Age of Leo by delving into the world of the Nile Valley. One of the deities that was inherited by the Kemites is Ta-Urt (meaning The Great One/feminine). In the Kemetic language, female names frequently end with a 't' sound. Ta-Urt is one of the oldest deities and precedes the establishment of Kemet (5500 BCE/BC) by thousands of years. In the picture of the sculpture on the previous page, we can see that she wears a Nubian wig, which was most commonly worn by women. She possesses pronounced breasts as does the Venus statues featured in the previous chapter. Although she has the head of a crocodile, she is mostly associated with a hippopotamus in the folklore of the Ancient Nile Valley. It was common for Nile Valley inhabitants to associate deities with animals based on the animals' behavior and appearance. Ta-Urt often appears as a pregnant hippopotamus. Hippopotami are known to be fierce defenders of their young. The symbol that she is holding with both hands is a hieroglyph for "protection". Early inhabitants of the Nile Valley did not buy-in to the notion of the "damsel in distress" or the helpless woman that was completely reliant upon man.

In the Nile Valley pantheon of deities, protection and the righteous path are often provided by female deities. This reality is also reflected in the burial practices of the Kemites, which are rooted in mythology that evolved over several Ages. For example the four sons of Heru carried the canopic jars that held the lungs, stomach, liver, and intestines into the next realm as a part of the burial process. The names of his four sons were Hapi, Duamutef, Imsety, and Qebehsenuef. Their mission was supported by the protection of four godesses: Nephthys, Neith, Auset, and Serqet.

Goddess MA'AT is also relevant to this subject. MA'AT symbolizes principles such as harmony, justice, propriety, balance, and order. Nile valley inhabitants personified her and presented her as a woman. She was also presented as a mixture of a woman and a vulture, an approach known as "composite" form. The fact that her zootype is a vulture tells us a lot. Usage of animals that were not abundantly present in the days of Kemet suggests that the animals and the cosmology originated from ancestors of the Kemites – in this case those ancestors were from the high lands further to the south where vegetation was more abundant and there was a wider spectrum of animal life. An important way to distinguish MA'AT from other deities is that MA'AT wears on her head the feather of an ostrich. In Ancient Kemetic mythology of the afterlife, a person's heart had to be lighter than the feather of MA'AT.

Ta-Urt, MA'AT, Nephthys, Neith, Auset, and Serqet each go back millennia before the establishment of the country of Ancient Egypt/Kemet. Collectively they reflect the

Image of MA'AT at Kom Ombo Temple, Egypt

Image of MA'AT at The Valley of the Kings in Thebes, Egypt

high regard that humanity had for feminine energy throughout the universe over the course of hundreds of thousands of years, through the Age of Leo, and going into the Age of Cancer.

The Age of Cancer (10,000-8,000 years ago) was a period of migration towards the Nile River away from the regions south and west of the Nile. The push factor was the drying out of the Sahara that occurred over thousands of years. Populations brought their own cosmologies and deities. One of the primary influences was the cosmology that came from the areas of contemporary Sudan and Ethiopia, which included the mythology of Ausar's resurrection. It is clear that this mythology was present in Nubia (contemporary Sudan) during the Age of Cancer and before Egypt was established. This fact is made clear by the Qustul incense burner that was found in the region before the building of the Aswan Dam that was finished in 1970. It was dated to be older than the Egyptian artifacts. The mythology of Ausar, Auset, and Heru was already in tact during the Age of Cancer.

The Qustul incense burner reveals a serekh (a.k.a. "façade") on its far right. It also shows a seated king with the crown of the "white crown" that would later be worn by Kemetic kings. This king represents Ausar – especially because he holds in his hand the flail that is associated with Ausar. To the left of the Ausar image is Heru, the son of Ausar, atop a serekh. I surmise that this symbolizes an actual king of those times because Nile Valley kings thought of themselves as Heru on Earth. That explains why Heru would be featured here standing atop a serekh, which symbolizes

The Qustul Incense Burner

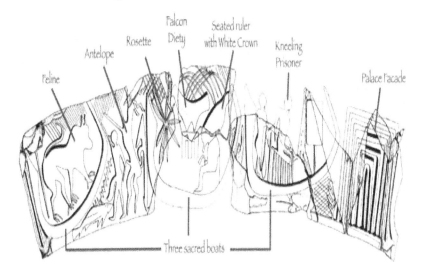

the home of the king. Further to the left is an antelope-like animal, which was not a part of the Kemetic landscape. This suggests that the incense burner is either from south of Kemet, the same region long before Kemet was established, or both. I believe both are likely. Furthermore, linguistic study makes it clear that the Kemetic language has its origins in the high lands of the Nile, which includes Sudan and Ethiopia.[2]

In the mythology of Ausar's resurrection, his bride Auset was cast as a (s)hero. She was so devoted that she

---

[2] For details of the Resurrection Story of Ausar and the linguistic evidence relating to the Nile Valley, see Chapter 3 of *Beyond Maafa*.

Ancient Egyptian Carving Auset and Heru

searched the world in search of Ausar, after he became a victim of his brother Set's selfishness. Despite formidable opposition, she ultimately succeeded in bringing Ausar back to life by breathing into his mouth. It is Auset who fashioned Ausar a new phallus after his ordeal with Set. According to Pyramid Text 1036, Auset cut off Heru's hand and fashioned

King Pepi ll in the lap of his mother Ankhnesmerira

him a new one after he was violated by Set. She was also the
protector of the boy Heru when his uncle, Set, sets out to kill

him. As we proceed through this processional cycle, it becomes more and more clear that the physical features of womanity were appreciated without shame or vulgarity. She is depicted as protector of child and compliment of man.

As the Ages have proceeded, more evidence becomes available, enabling us to piece together a clearer picture. By the time of the Age of Gemini (8,000-6,000 years ago) a clash of civilizations was emerging. The positive presentation of feminine energy in general was sustained in the regions that still practiced cultures that were consistent with our original human cultures. The image above is a sculpture of Auset and her son Heru. This was a common representation of Auset and Heru, with Auset breastfeeding the baby Heru. During the Age of Gemini one of the most powerful men that ever existed in human history up to that time was Pepi II, who was the last great king of the Kemetic Old Kingdom. In the image above, Pepi II is depicted with his mother in the classic posturing of Auset and Heru. The cultural norms that were still practiced along the Nile at that time were Southern Cradle cultural norms. Southern Cradle norms emphasized complementarity between man and woman. Their primary source of food was agriculture, which meant that men, women, and children all took part in the process of food cultivation and preparation.

The Southern Cradle culture experienced a great culture clash with the cultures that emerged from the Northern Cradle. Northern Cradle cultures have a Eurasian origin. Their cultures revolved around hunting and women were devalued. When all the pieces are put together, it appears that the formation of the country of Kemet and its increasing focus on militarization was inspired by the desire to fend off the Northern Cradle cultures. I come to this conclusion based on a number of pieces of evidence from the Ages of Gemini and Taurus. The Narmer Palette was used to mix make-up and survived from the times of Narmer, one of the first kings of Kemet. The palette tells the story of Narmer consolidating the Kemetic control of the region and also subduing foreigners. Additionally *The Instruction of Merikare*, a work of literature from the latter years of the Age of Gemini, reveals the necessity of having to stave off the "Asiatics". The story makes reference to the inspiration of the Asiatics, who emerged from a resource-poor environment. *The Instruction of Merikare* states, "...the Asiatic is a crocodile on its shore, It snatches from a lonely road, It cannot seize from a populous town." The sum of the evidence clearly reveals that this clash of civilizations and the amoral aggression of the Northern Cradle over the years were linked to their limited intellectual and natural resources. This would also be the case for the misogyny that emerged from the Northern Cradle. This reality was clear to the Roman scholar Pliny the Elder in 77 AD when he wrote in his book *Natural History* "while the latter [speaking of the Northern Cradle] are fierce owing to the rigidity of their climate but the former [meaning the Ethiopians] are wise owing to the mobility of theirs."

The Age of Gemini was a turning point in human history. During this Age, the contours of this great culture clash began to take form. Henceforth, the greatest threat to the Southern Cradle was the ambitions of the Northern Cradle and their decadent culture that bred sexism and misogyny.

Martial training in the tomb of Khnumhotep II at Beni Hasan, Egypt. Khnumhotep II was a popular 12th Dynasty political figure. His tomb is a very fruitful historical resource for scholars.

During the Age of Taurus (6,000-4,000 ya) militarization increased in the Nile Valley and the land of Sumer/Mesopotamia, as traditional Africoid populations were increasingly threatened by the Asiatic world. Military training became more formalized in Kemet as the scale of warfare increased and defense efforts against foreign threats increased during the era. During this era, about 2,300 BCE, the Black civilization of Sumer was established by the Akkadians. They too conceived of the Almighty as having a female compliment. Mother goddesses like Asherah were passed on to Canaanite populations from them.

The Age of Aries (4,000-2,000 years ago) was a turning point in the regions of the Mediterranean that were eventually engulfed by the Northern Cradle. This reality is most apparent among the Hebrews of Ancient Israel. The "books" of the *Old Testament* have their foundation in the Ancient Hebrew texts that were passed to them in the mythology of the Semitic branch of the Ethiopic/Afro-Asiatic language family. These groups include Canaanite descendants such as the Hebrews and the Carthaginians.

As the Ethiopic cultural/linguistic group proliferated throughout the Mediterranean Sea, they held no preoccupation with the notion that God (meaning a singular, Almighty, Most High) was the only god. They acknowledged the presence of God in lesser divinities and also had multiple names for God. This point is made clear throughout the line of texts that led to the creation of the *King James Bible*. This mythology that had been passed down orally for hundreds and possibly thousands of years had come to be expressed in Hebrew by 800 BCE. The passage that has come to be known as Genesis 1:1 was stated in the ancient Hebrew texts as, "In the beginning [Elohim] created the heavens and the earth," - not "God" created the heavens. Throughout the Canaanite world "El" referred to the single Almighty/Most High. To express plurality the word "Elohim" was used. In this instance "Elohim" was a veiled reference to various aspects of the Almighty in similar fashion to the Kemetic and Yoruba cosmologies.

"Elohim" also referred to the Hebrew pantheon of deities. For example in Deuteronomy 10:17 of the *King James Bible* the word "Elohim" was replaced with "God" and the word "Yahweh" was replaced with "Lord". In its original Hebrew form before the decline of Judea the passage would read more like "For [Yahweh] your [Elohim] is [Elohim] of all [Elohim]" instead of "For the Lord your God is God of Gods." In their conceptualization there was interplay between the gods.

One of the deities in this pantheon was Asherah who was a prototypical "Mother Goddess" in the cosmology and mythology of the ancient Hebrews. Asherah was also featured in the pantheon of deities of other Canaanite peoples. Over the course of recent decades, artifacts have been found that illustrate the worship of Asherah in Israel. Like other Mother Goddesses her femininity was celebrated. Her figurines could be used to generate desired outcomes such as a robust harvest or fertility in the human reproductive sense. It was common for temples in the world of the ancient Israelites to grace images of Asherah. Various inscriptions of those ancient times list Asherah as the compliment/consort/wife of the Almighty "Yahweh".

Asherah holding a child, reminiscent of Auset and Mary, mother of Jesus. National Maritime Museum, Israel - Terracotta Figure

Image of Mother Goddess found in at a Tel Aviv, Israel archaeological site called Tell Qasile.

For more information read Amihai Mazar's paper titled "POTTERY PLAQUES DEPICTING GODDESSES STANDING IN TEMPLE FACADES" in the *Michmanim* 85, 2 published by the Reuben and Edith Hecht Museum at Haifa University.

It was very common for ancient Hebrews to associate Yahweh with another goddess by the name of Sophia. "Sophia" was the personification of the "wisdom". Dozens of "books" that were not included into the King James Version of *The Holy Bible* reveal this special relationship between Yahweh and a consort. For example, in the Wisdom of Solomon the protagonist pleads to Yahweh:

> Give me Wisdom, who sits enthroned beside you...send her out to me from your holy heavens. Send her from your glorious throne so that she may labor with me here and that I may learn what is pleasing to you.[3]

Note the Sophia, or wisdom, is not cast as a subordinate deity – she is on the throne along with Yahweh, or God as he has come to be known. This relationship becomes clearer when the book of Proverbs is read in this light. Sophia/Wisdom proclaimed:

> The Lord created me at the beginning of his work, the first of his acts of old. Ages ago I was set up, at the first before the beginning of the earth...when he established the heavens I was there......when he marked out the foundations of the earth, then I was beside him, like a master workman.[4]

---

[3] *Wisdom of Solomon*: 8, 4-10

[4] The above passage from Proverbs 8, 22-30 was quoted from April D. Deconick's *Holy Misogyny: Why the Sex and Gender Conflicts in the Early Church Still Matter*. I quoted from this text because the translation in text is closer to the original Hebrew texts than the *KJV Holy Bible*.

Thus Sophia was co-partner in the building and ordering of the universe.

So why has the presence of wisdom as Sophia, Asherah as divine mother, and both of them as the consort of Yahweh been stricken from the orthodox texts or hidden in plain sight? The answer is that the Hebrew scholars under the rule of the Babylonians were forced to modify the ancient texts to suit the political objectives of the Babylonian overseers. This reality occurred over a couple centuries. By the 6th century BCE there arose debates within the Hebrew priestly class that can be characterized as monotheism vs. monolatry. Monotheism refers to the worship of only one god, who is *the* Supreme Being. Monolatry is the worship of one Supreme Being while not denying the existence of other gods.

The major turning point was the conquering of the nation of Judah in 586 BCE by the Babylonians. This was not an isolated conflict – it involved other nations throughout the region including Assyria and Egypt. To achieve their objectives the Babylonians defeated the Egyptians, who were their primary rivals. The Babylonians began the process of creating a class of Hebrew leaders to protect their interests in Judah. This group of leaders had a great challenge before them. They needed to reproduce a corpus of religious documents from the limited documents that survived the turmoil of war. They needed to preserve the preeminence of Yahweh and yet, explain why Yahweh had enabled them to be conquered. In essence, the worship of Asherah, Sophia, and other deities was the perfect scapegoat. Yahweh's anger over the worship of these deities explained torment they

Judah faced in the doctored Hebrew literature that was sanitized by the Babylonians. Had they only praised Yahweh and no others, then Yahweh would not have forsaken them. This enabled them to preserve their religious faith without offending Babylonian sensibilities, all while maintaining the individual supremacy of Yahweh. This was also the context in which the Kemites, who were not historical rivals or enslavers of the Ancient Hebrews, began to be characterized as oppressors in the sanitized Hebrew literature that began to emerge after Babylonian rule.

As I argued in the first chapter of this text, misogyny as we know has its origins in the European world. During the Age of Aries (4,000-2,000 years ago) European imperialism resulted in the diffusion of the anti-woman culture of the Greeks and the Romans. The Greeks were the first of the European countries to come into the civilized world, largely due to their tutelage under the Ancient Egyptians. However this relationship could not eradicate their long established tradition of misogyny. It was a common belief among Greeks that the immoral man reincarnated as a woman and that a woman is a physically and emotionally underdeveloped man. Sexual exploitation of non-citizen men, women, boys, and girls was commonly accepted behavior in Greek society.

The misogynist aspect of Greek sexual depravity is reflected in Greek mythology. In Greek mythology the first Earthly woman that was created was named Pandora. Pandora was created by the lord of the Greek gods, Zeus, as a

According to Greek mythology, man's suffering is attributed to Pandora opening the box against the will of Zeus, the king of the gods.

punishment to man. It came to be accepted in Greek mythology that Pandora was responsible for all the hardships faced by humanity. Greek concepts regarding sex relations foreshadowed what was to come in the Piscean Age.

The Greeks did not infect the world of the Mediterranean with this value system on a large scale. Greek imperialism was limited in large part because the Greeks could not dedicate many military forces to foreign locations since their primary domestic threat was the slaves that they subjugated at home in Greece. The advances that the Greeks made under the conqueror Alexander were cut short by Alexander's sudden death at age thirty-three.

In the subsequent Age, which was the Piscean Age, the Romans colonized much of Asia, Africa, and nearly all of Europe. Along with them came a tsunami of rape, imperialism, and misogyny. In Ancient Roman culture, rape and homosexuality were linked. Rape and sodomy were parts of the colonization process and used as a method to further subjugate conquered peoples. It was forbidden to rape Roman citizens, yet acceptable to rape slaves and non-citizens of either sex. Adult males could "evolve" past being sexually subjugated as he rose in authority and standing. The Romans seemed to have a preoccupation with gay sex. Although they lusted after male and female children, they commonly ridiculed gay males. This mindset was common, even amongst those that participated in some type of gay sex.

The Piscean Age includes the past 2,000 years of human history, roughly beginning with the era of Jesus' supposed birth. Rome's arrival on the world stage as a superpower in 201 BCE had grievous consequences for the populations within their sphere of influence. For the last two hundred years of the BCE era and nearly the first 500 years of Piscean Age, Rome was the dominant political and military power throughout the Mediterranean.

It is safe to say that Rome hijacked the Christian religion by wrestling it away from the original Christians of the Mediterranean. The word "Christian" was coined by a Gnostic priest by the name of Valentinus. Gnostics held no singular set of beliefs. The closest thing to a unifying belief among Gnostics was the belief that the ultimate goal of "Gnosis", which is akin to "salvation", "consciousness", or "awakening", was accomplished by way of knowledge and self-discipline. Valentinus was likely born in Alexandria, Egypt and became a hugely influential teacher throughout Alexandria, Egypt in the 2nd century CE/AD.

Valentinus' conceptualization of creation centralized the deity Sophia. Gnostic mythology tended to focus more so on the theme of redemption, whereas those that argued that Jesus' birth was literal focused on sin and hierarchy. Furthermore, Valentinus believed in a complementarity system of deities where each deity was complimented by the opposite sex. This system is akin to that of the Dogon of West Africa, the Ancient Egyptians, and other African cosmological systems. The Gnostics were by no means "feminist" in the contemporary sense; however they did not see the need to mute the voices of women that were teachers. Valentinus was criticized widely by the priests of the 2nd and 3rd centuries CE who are now regarded as "Church Fathers" of the Catholics. Among these men was Tertullian, who declared:

All are puffed up, all offer you knowledge. Their catechumens are perfect before they are fully taught. The very women of these heretics, how wanton they are! For they are bold enough to teach, to dispute, to enact exorcisms, to undertake cures – it may be even to baptize.[5]

These practices contrasted Greco-Roman cultural norms whereby the domain of respectable women was the home, and certainly not the political or religious sphere. In the world of Rome, women held no voting rights and no legal recourse outside of that which was afforded by her husband. Thus the practices of Valentinus and his followers challenged the foundations of Roman cultural beliefs.

Since the Gnostics were the last bastion of uncorrupted Cristian thought, I will present here some Gnostic perspectives on two of the popular themes within Christianity. Those themes are 1) the Trinity and 2) the Adam and Eve story. The body of Gnostic texts presents a concept of the Trinity that is in accord with their geographical and ideological "parents", who were the Ancient Egyptians. The Kemetic Trinity was Ausar the father, Auset the mother, and Heru the child. As I stated earlier in this chapter, Auset was cast a "shero", meaning a female hero. The Gnostic corpus of literature held no single set of beliefs or cosmologies, however their literature commonly featured a man, woman, and child as the Trinity. This approach was taken by the Valentinians and their Gnostic counterparts, the Sethians.

---

[5] Anne McGuire, "Women, Gender, and Gnosis In Gnostic Texts Traditions", in *Women and Christian Origins*, (Oxford: Oxford University Press, 1999), pg. 246.

An image of Eve with a "serpent" wrapped around her.

Experts credit the Sethians as the authors of the *Trimorphic Protennoia*, which literally translates into English as "The First Thought Which Is In Three Forms". In the *Trimorphic Protennoia* God speaks in the first person to convey God's preeminence, sometimes self-clarifying as "man" and other times "woman". God exhorts, "Now the Voice that originated from my Thought exists as three permanencies: the Father, the Mother, the Son".

During the first centuries of the Piscean Age those within the Christian world debated the true nature of Jesus. In 325 CE Emperor Constantine of Rome organized the First Council of Nicea in modern-day Turkey. The prevailing perspective was that God, Jesus, and the Holy Spirit were "of the same substance". Henceforth the Catholic Church propogated the doctrine that the Trinity was the Father, the Son, and the Holy Spirit.[6] Although each of the three has come to be recognized as masculine in church teachings, it is known by a few that in the Hebrew origin of the "Holy Spirit", "spirit" is feminine.

The tone of the Adam and Eve story is significantly different in the Gnostic literature from the Catholic doctrine that was canonized at their various council meetings. In one of the Gnostic texts called *The Hypostasis of the Archons*, the Adam and Eve story is far more nuanced that the Roman

---

[6] Even though the wicked alliance between Constantine and the Catholic Church resulted in the purging of a Trinity that included a divine mother, texts still arose that spoke to the history of the divine mother in Christian theology. A theologian by the name of Jerome visited Antioch in modern-day Syria 372 CE and during his visit he came across a document that has come to be known as the *Gospel of the Hebrews*. In this text Jesus exclaims, "My mother the Holy Spirit took me by one of the hairs on my head and bore me off to the great mountain Tabor."

Catholic version. In this version, Sophia is consistently present in the form of an exalted creator. The snake comes in the form of a nurturing mother, however in it represents the "authorities of darkness". The text is clearly abstract and not to be taken literally. Although God punishes Adam and Eve, the tone is considerably different. One of the primary reasons why is that the authors of the texts did not seek to use the text to promote the notion that women embodied sin.

The version of the Adam and Eve story that was passed down by the Roman Catholic Church is preoccupied with maintaining hierarchy. In Genesis Chapter Two, God made Adam and from Adam's rib came Eve. Inculcated in this event is the value of male dominion over woman. Note that this is a deviation away from Genesis Chapter One where both man and woman are created by God. In fact, Chapter One, Verse 26 states, "Let [US] make man in [OUR] image", which did not imply of a single, male God. Furthermore, Chapter 1, Verse 27 states, "So God created man in his image, in the image of God crated he him; male and female created he them". In verse 27 the subordination of womanity is not suggested. However the tone changes considerably in Chapter 2. Chapter 2 emphasizes hierarchy as opposed to "goodness" as in Chapter 1. There is one sole omnipotent God in Chapter 2. He created Eve from Adam's rib. In Chapter 2 God communicates to Adam that "thou shalt not eat of" the "tree of knowledge". Eve's decision to eat from the "trees in the midst of the garden" and Adam's decision to follow her results in "enmity between man and woman", painful conception for all women, and hardened soil to till for Adam. The tone here reinforces the notion of a wrathful

God and is considerably different in tone from the Gnostic texts. Chapter 3, Verse 16 reaffirms man's hierarchical rule over woman when God states to Eve, "thy desire shall be to thy husband, and he shall rule over thee". This interpretation of the Adam and Eve story reinforced the misogyny in the domestic, political, and legal norms of the Roman world.

By the time that Athanasius gathered the texts that would become the New Testament in 315 CE, these texts included the 1 Timothy 2: 8-15 passage, which encouraged the subordination of women:

> Therefore I want the men everywhere to pray, lifting up holy hands without anger or disputing. I also want the women to dress modestly, with decency and propriety, adorning themselves, not with elaborate hairstyles or gold or pearls or expensive clothes, but with good deeds, appropriate for women who profess to worship God. A woman should learn in quietness and full submission. I do not permit a woman to teach or to assume authority over a man; she must be quiet. For Adam was formed first, then Eve. And Adam was not the one deceived; it was the woman who was deceived and became a sinner. But women will be saved through childbearing—if they continue in faith, love and holiness with propriety.

During the Piscean Age Roman cultural norms of misogyny and rape spread like wildfire. So did the church doctrine that sought to eradicate the practice of women teaching in public. "Inspired" texts served to reinforce values in the form of scripture that were established with the sword.

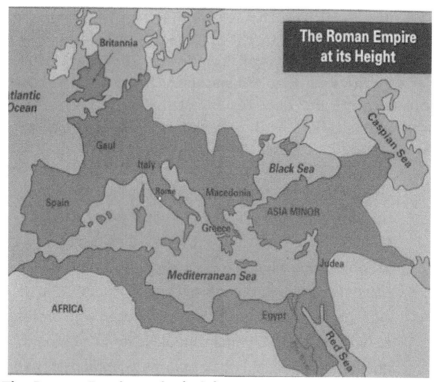

The Roman Empire at its height.

Chapter 3

How The Divine Mother Became White

This chapter addresses Mary's transformation to pristine whiteness at the behest of the Catholic Church. Not only did she become white, she also become passive, and near silent. In essence she fit right in with a world that went to exhaustive measures to subjugate women.

As proven in Chapter 2, there was a systematic purging of women from the clergy and an erasure of scripture passages that present women in positions of authority. However before and during this time, Mary had a cosmological, symbolic, and mythological purpose. She was not simply thought to be a "historical" person. For example, the *Gospel of Philip*, which is a Gnostic text, mentions that:

> There were three walking with the Lord all the time. Mary his mother and her sister and Magdalene, the woman who was called his partner. For "Mary" was his sister and his mother and his partner.

Before we delve into Mary the mother, it is necessary to understand the story of Mary Magdalene and why we know so little about her.

Image of Mary Magdalene announcing the Resurrection of Jesus to the Apostles. England St. Albans Abbey, England, 1119-1123.

Mary Magdalene

Just like Jesus, Mary Magdalene is a victim of one the greatest character assassinations in human history. One of the details regarding her is that she is acknowledged in Matthew and John as a person who went to Jesus' tomb, only to find that his body was not there. Mary exclaimed to Jesus other disciples, "They have taken the Lord out of the tomb, and we don't know where they have put him!" Upon returning to the tomb she was approached by Jesus but did not initially recognize him:

> [14] At this, she turned around and saw Jesus standing there, but she did not realize that it was Jesus. [15] He asked her, "Woman, why are you crying? Who is it you are looking for?" Thinking he was the gardener, she said, "Sir, if you have carried him away, tell me where you have put him, and I will get him." [16] Jesus said to her, "Mary." She turned toward him and cried out in Aramaic, "Rabboni!" (which means "Teacher").[1]

Mary Magdalene was thought to be Jesus' favored disciple and follower. For example In the *Gospel of Mary Magdalene*, a Gnostic text is written in the 2nd century, Mary was asked by Peter to, "Tell us the words of the Savior which you remember which you know, but we do not, nor have we heard them. Mary answered and said, 'What is hidden from you I will proclaim to you.'" A few took exception to her commentary, including Peter, who exhorted, "Are we to turn about and all listen to her? Did He prefer her to us?" In

---

[1] Book of John, 20:11-16, *KJV*.

response Levi commented:

> Levi answered and said to Peter, Peter you have always been hot tempered. Now I see you contending against the woman like the adversaries. But if the Savior made her worthy, who are you indeed to reject her? Surely the Savior knows her very well. That is why He loved her more than us.

It should come as no surprise that the *Gospel of Mary* was hidden during the Roman purge. The passage possesses two Gnostic cultural norms that the Historicists wanted to eradicate.[2] The first norm is the female teacher, which by teaching *to* men, assumes a position of authority over men. The other is the female prophet to whom Jesus spoke through – thus placing her *over* the men.

Mary Magdalene is also conceptualized as Jesus' female compliment. In the *Gospel of Philip*, she is Jesus companion: "...the partner of [Jesus the Savior] is Mary Magdalene. The [Savior loved] her more than all of the disciples, and often he kissed her on her [mouth]." The text also includes a passage that is quite telling of early Christian thought before the purge: "When we were Hebrews, we were orphans and had only our mother, but when we became Christians, we had both father and mother."

Mary Magdalene – teacher, prophetess, and compliment of Jesus – represented everything the burgeoning Catholic Church stood against. During the first six

---

[2] The Historicists who believed and/or argued that it was an actual fact that Jesus Christ came to Earth as a physical man and was physically resurrected. They propagate the argument that the King James Holy Bible is a history book.

centuries of the Piscean Age, the Historicists went to work on Magdalene's image, mischaracterizing her as a whore. But why a whore? Although she is cast as a repentant whore, even a redeemed whore carried a stigma that could never be eradicated. Furthermore, it went hand in hand with the Historicist's modification of the scripture, which cast Jesus as single and denounced the overly conversant woman as a whore. An example is the condemnation of Jezebel in Revelations 10:20-23:

> **20** Nevertheless, I have this against you: You tolerate that woman Jezebel, who calls herself a prophet. By her teaching she misleads my servants into sexual immorality and the eating of food sacrificed to idols. **21** I have given her time to repent of her immorality, but she is unwilling. **22** So I will cast her on a bed of suffering, and I will make those who commit adultery with her suffer intensely, unless they repent of her ways. **23** I will strike her children dead.

In order to bestow upon Mary Magdalene the permanent designation of repentant whore, the Historicist ascribed passages to her that supported this character assassination. In Luke 7:36-39, Jesus visits the home of a Hebrew where he makes the acquaintance of a female "sinner":

36 When one of the Pharisees invited Jesus to have dinner with him, he went to the Pharisee's house and reclined at the table. **37** A woman in that town who lived a sinful life learned that Jesus was eating at the Pharisee's house, so she came there with an alabaster jar of perfume. **38** As she stood behind him at his feet weeping, she began to wet his feet with her tears. Then she wiped them with her hair, kissed them and poured perfume on them. **39** When the Pharisee who had invited him saw this, he said to himself, "If this man were a prophet, he would know who is touching him and what kind of woman she is—that she is a sinner."

The Historicists fervently promoted the notion that the woman in the above passage was Mary Magdalene even though there is no evidence to support that claim. Furthermore, other Gospel passages that feature a "Mary" drying Jesus' feet with her hair is ascribed to Magdalene. Why? Because this shows subordination and submission, unlike the St. Albany image above that features her waiving the right hand of a teacher. Mary Magdalene's fate was sealed by 591 CE when Pope Gregory claimed that:

> She whom Luke calls the sinful woman, whom John calls Mary, we believe to be the Mary from whom seven devils were ejected according to Mark. And what did these seven devils signify, it not all the vices...the woman previously used the unguent to perfume her flesh in forbidden acts. What she

therefore displayed more scandalously, she was now offering to God in a more praiseworthy manner. She had coveted with earthly eyes, but now through penitence these are consumed with tears. She displayed her hair to set off her face, but now here hair dries her tears. She had spoken proud things with her mouth, but in kissing the Lord's feet, she now planted her mouth on the Redeemer's feet...

This declaration by Pope Gregory further illustrates the ineffectiveness of the *Holy Bible* as a history book. This claim is further discredited by the fact that 23.4 % of Jewish women in Palestine between 330 BCE and 200 CE had the name Mary. Of the women mentioned in the New Testament, 42.5 % of the women are named "Mary".[3]

Magdalene's response to Peter's request to share the savior's message does add more insight. She exhorted:

"Again it came to the third power, which is called ignorance. [It (the power)] questioned the soul saying, 'Where are you going? In wickedness are you bound. But you are bound; do not judge!' And the soul said, 'why do you judge me although I have not judged? I was bound though I have not bound. I was not recognized. But I have recognized that the All is being dissolved, both the earthly (things) and the heavenly.'

[3] Jane Schaberg, *The Resurrection of Mary Magdalene: Legends, Apocrypha, and the Christian Testament*, (Continuum International Publishing Group: New York, 2002), pgs. 66-67.

When the soul had overcome the third power, it went upwards and saw the fourth power, (which) took seven forms. The first form is darkness, the second desire, the third ignorance, the fourth is the excitement of death, the fifth is the kingdom of the flesh, the sixth is the foolish wisdom of flesh, the seventh is the wrathful wisdom. These are the seven [powers] of wrath. They ask the soul, 'Whence do you come, slayer of men, or where are you going, conqueror of space?' The soul answered and said, 'What binds me has been slain, and what surrounds me has been overcome, and my desire has been ended, and ignorance has died. In a [world] I was released from a world, [and] in a type from a heavenly type, and (from) the fetter of oblivion which is transient. From this time on will I attain to the rest of the time, of the season, of the aeon, in silence.'

This passage represented everything the Historicist stood against in three flagrant ways: 1) the passage champions knowledge over faith 2) a female establishing authority of males 3) a woman establishes herself as a prophetess.

By design or by tradition, the common understanding of Mary Magdalene amongst the multitudes has unfortunately become that of a repentant whore instead of a foremost disciple of Jesus Christ.

The Creation of the Virgin Mother

Immaculate Conception was not a new concept in Rome by the time of the first centuries of the CE era. The Cult of Auset had been a popular religious group throughout the Mediterranean. The Roman Emperor Vaspasian frequented various Egyptian spiritualists before and after his seizure of Rome in 69 CE. One of the temples that he visited was the Temple of Auset. Additionally we know that the Sana Maria sopra Minerva, one of the major churches in Rome, was built directly over a Temple of Auset. Auset's Immaculate Conception occurred after Auset miraculously brought Ausar back to life. She fashioned Ausar a phallus, which was the only part of his body that was missing after his reassembling. The virgin Auset then took part in an Immaculate Conception by conceiving with Ausar. Thus, her son Heru was not necessarily born to a virgin.

During Rome's Second Punic War against Hannibal and the Carthaginians, the Roman Senate appealed to Cybele, a great mother goddess that was introduced to them by Attulus I of Pergamum in 205 BCE. Attulus sent the statue, whose head was a black stone, to which the Romans called upon under threat of defeat by Carthage. The mythology associated with Cybele's impregnation involves forced sex and accidental insemination, but not quite the miraculous impregnation by the Almighty without the seed of an earthly male.

The notion of a Divine Mother that was an outright virgin is a consequence of a myriad of rapidly changing circumstances in the Christian world from the 2nd century CE to fairly recent times. Before the 2nd and 3rd centuries Roman religious laws were relaxed. The rigid, restrictive doctrine and law that was forced upon the Roman world intensified in the 3rd century and set the tone for hundreds of years to come. All religious doctrine that undermined the Catholic

Church's teachings was systematically erased.[4] Within the expansive Mediterranean empire of Rome were countless peoples whose cultures relied on the bounty and fortune that was provided by a mother goddess. To these masses, the Virgin Mary was their last and only hope at connecting with the divine mother goddess.

The Virgin Mary replaced the longing for Cybele, Auset, Asherah, and other mother goddesses. Pagan beliefs and customs die hard, even when faced with the prospect of death. To the masses the Virgin Mother enabled the perpetual worship of the feminine principle in a way that suited their sensibilities, all while not standing out in the Roman purge of all contradictory doctrines. The contrived Virgin Mary narrative served the Catholic Church by de-sexualizing the mother goddess. Unlike the other mother goddesses, she did not conceive by way of sexual intercourse with a human. Therefore, her example contrasted the characterization of Mary Magdalene as a whore, and also contrasted Auset and Cybele, whereas both of them were deflowered in a more earthly sense. Furthermore, the Virgin Mary served the purpose of bringing uniformity to the vast terrain of the Roman Empire.

At the Council of Ephesus in 431 CE, Mary's title of "Mother of God" became accepted as doctrine by the Catholic Church. This gathering concerned the contrasting views of two factions within the church. One was a faction led by Nestorius, who was the Archbishop of Constantinople (contemporary Turkey). Nestorians promoted the belief that Mary gave birth to a man of flesh that came embodied

---

[4] For more on the process of eradicating "heretical" literature by Rome see Perry Kyles' *The Book That Every Black Christian Should Read*.

"Christ". On the contrary, Cyril, who was Patriarch of Alexandria argued that Jesus was *always* wholly man and *wholly* divine. Cyril prevailed and so did the notion of a Virgin Mother that was not deflowered by man, and who in turn, remained a virgin even after the arrival of Jesus Christ. This perspective was reinforced at the Council of Chalcedon in 451 AD. Thus, it became the official position of the church that the Virgin Mary, "Mother of God" was the sole legitimate mother goddess.

The Mother Goddesses pulled off a great feat by surviving the tsunami of misogyny that was actively promoted during the last three centuries of the Roman Empire. In a sense her position as the primordial womb became even more apparent by her title "Theotokos", which translates from Greek to English as "Mother of God". Throughout Europe's Dark Ages (roughly 500-1500 CE) there was scarcely a community that did not ascribe either implicitly or explicitly to the worship of Virgin Mary. The Black Madonna, the Virgin Mary, and the "Theotokos" were all popularized by the union of the Roman church and state. Additionally the Goths that toppled Rome in 410 CE worshipped Virgin Mary and propagated the worship of Virgin Mary in regions under their dominion. In his authoritative work *The Cult of the Black Virgin* Ian Begg states that the Christian Visigoths "accelerated the decline of paganism in the lands they controlled and the transition to the Christian Goddess."[5]

According to the folklore associated with the Virgin of Montseratt statue, it originated from Jerusalem. The three

---

[5] Ian Begg, *The Cult of the Black Virgin*, pg. 20

Virgin of Montserrat (Spain)

foot high wooden statue was brought to the Catalonia region
in 718 in an effort to hide her from invading Muslims.
Supposedly a Goth bishop hid her and she was eventually

Virgin of Czestochowa

found by shepherds in a mountain cave in 888. Note that baby Jesus sits in the lap of his mother. The Virgin of Czestochowa also carries an interesting folklore. Legend has it that she was painted by St. Luke over a cedar table in the home of Mary and Jesus. The legend continues that St. Helen, mother of the Emperor Constantine, found it in Jerusalem and brought it to Constantinople in the year 326 CE. Her presence was known to have compelled enemy troupes to retreat. In 802 it was moved to Russia and by 1382 it was held in Czestochowa, Poland where it continues to receive droves of annual visitors.

Another aspect that influenced the perpetuation of Black Madonna worship is the advance of the Knights Templar that was founded in 1129. The official name of the Templars is *The Poor Fellow-Soldiers of Christ and of the Temple of Solomon.* They were an order of Christian knights that were sworn to live a life of limited financial means and strict religious precepts. The Templars traversed the Old World, working as escorts and providing financial services to pilgrims seeking to visit Jerusalem. While there is mystery surrounding their initiation rites, it is largely accepted that the Templars practiced a Gnostic variant of Christianity that included the worship of Mary Magdalene along with Virgin Mary. Furthermore, they played a part in the movement of Black Madonna statues throughout the Old World.

The Emergence of the White Madonna

Over the course of the Piscean Age the popular Virgin Mary imagery of the church became increasingly white or European in terms of her features. This shift is by no means coincidental. It coincides with the emergence of race hierarchy in the European race to exploit Africa and the Americas. A major event that fueled this regression was the signing of the Treaty of Tordesillas in 1494. The treaty was brokered by Pope Alexander VI who essentially split the New Lands between Spain and Portugal.

The discussion of Spain's and Portugal's "discovery" of the New World has been addressed in every curriculum on Earth. Here I'll just reiterate some of their objectives. They were in the midst of an ongoing clash of civilizations with the Muslim world. Spain in particular had only been free of Moorish rule for two years after being under Moorish rule since 711 CE. These two states saw the colonization of the lands that were signed over to them by the Treaty of Tordesillas as a path to riches and a reliable war chest.

Just as the Romans had done to their very ancestors, the Spaniards in the Americas brought forth their own blend of violence and rape. Columbus wrote to King Ferdinand of Portugal:

> As soon as I arrived in the Indies, in the first island which I found, I took some of the natives by force, in order that they might learn and might give me information of whatever there is in these parts. And so it was that they soon understood us, and we them, either by speech or by signs, and they have been very serviceable.

Michele da Cuneo, an acquaintance of Columbus who accompanied him wrote in a 1495 letter:

> While I was in the boat, I captured a very beautiful Carib woman, whom the said Lord Admiral gave to me. When I had taken her to my cabin she was

naked—as was their custom. I was filled with a desire to take my pleasure with her and attempted to satisfy my desire. She was unwilling, and so treated me with her nails that I wished I had never begun. But—to cut a long story short—I then took a piece of rope and whipped her soundly, and she let forth such incredible screams that you would not have believed your ears. Eventually we came to such terms, I assure you, that you would have thought that she had been brought up in a school for whores.

Disease, violence, and the sorrow of dehumanization decimated the Native American populations. From 1519 to 1608 the Native population of Mexico went from 20,000,000 to 1,000,000.[6] Bartalome de las Casas was a Spanish clergyman that took part in the Spanish seizure of Cuba in 1513 and ultimately owned several slaves. De las Casas began what became a very successful campaign to divert the enslavement of American Natives to the enslavement of Africans in the Americas. Towards the later years of his life, some fifty years later De las Casas denounced the enslavement of Africans but it was far too late.

Over the course of the 16th century the Spaniards and Portuguese began to focus their efforts on the capturing and enslavement of Africans from the territories that were signed over to Portugal by the Tordesillas Treaty.[7] Colonization and slavery began to take on a racialized tone

---

[6] Jared Diamond, *Guns, Germs, Steel: The Fate of Human Societies*, (New York: 1997), pg. 210.

[7] For a more detailed account of European enslavement of Africans see Chapter Seven of Perry Kyles' *Beyond Maafa: Black History From Human Origins to Recent Times*, (Houston: 2017).

bThe Madonna of the Pinks was painted by Italian painter Raphael about the year 1506.

unlike Roman slavery. Thus the Catholic Church, who was the centralizing force of all of Europe for several hundred years, could not publically worship the very same woman who was a daily victim of the brutality and rape perpetrated by Spaniards. The Church promoted a hierarchy based on power, sex, and race. "Black" increasingly became denigrated and associated with inferiority.

Over the course of the 16th century Madonna got whiter, especially as she related to the public representation of the *Theotokos*. During the first two centuries of European colonization of the Atlantic world, the race hierarchy concept solidified. It was fueled by the prospects of immense wealth and fame. By creating God in their own images and likenesses, it was a given that God would ordain their brutal rulership over Blacks, Browns, and Reds. Their movement fared better with the public consumption of the White Madonna, instead of a Black reminder of who Mary and Jesus *really* are. Just as the Kongo became engulfed by the wildfire of European expansion, a brave young soul took it upon herself to reclaim the original divine mother. We'll take up the story of Kimpa Vita in the next chapter.

Chapter 4

The Suppression of the Black Madonna

This chapter lays out the secret worship of the Black Madonna by the Roman Catholic Church, all while publicly presenting the Virgin Mary as a white woman. This reality has been purposely been blurred by church officials over the course of hundreds of years. However, with just a little bit of digging, it is quite possible to unravel the secret worship of the Black Madonna. That challenge is taken up in this chapter. The story of Kimpa Vita will put into perspective how western Europeans spread the same rampant violence and misogyny throughout the Atlantic world, just as the Romans had done to them centuries earlier. In true revolutionary fashion, Kimpa Vita deployed all available resources to repel their advance.

The Plight of Kimpa Vita (1684-1706)

Vita was born in 1684 to a high ranking family. The Kongo was among the regions that were devastated by war when Vita was born. Vita claimed that in 1704 she received visions of St. Anthony. According to Vita, she died and when she arose again, St. Anthony had overtaken her body. There is speculation that her connection with St. Anthony may be tied to King Antonio I of the Kongo who ruled from 1661-1665. This speculation is attributed to several factors. For one, his Kikongo name is Vita a Nkanga, thus there is the possibility

Drawing of the great spiritualist and leader Kimpa Vita. (1684-1706)

that they genetically, or culturally linked and that this was a meaningful commonality in her mind. Both Antonio I and Kimpa Vita fought to stabilize the region in the name of the Kingdom of Kongo. Although it cannot be proven for certain, it appears more likely that Kimpa Vita's spiritual connection with "Anthony" was more so linked with Anthony/Vita a

Nkanga whom she would have had a genetic, cultural, national, or even ideological connection.

Kimpa Vita built a large following of thousands and succeeded in reestablishing Sao Salvador, which was the former capital that had been destroyed. Her nationalist teachings were attractive to peoples whose communities had been ravished by civil war, and who were under the watchful eye of the Portuguese, who salivated at the prospects of vulnerable people to enslave. Vita taught that both Jesus and Mary were both Kongolese. Kimpa Vita strove to bring the Kongo under one king, and overcome the fragmentation that made them vulnerable to foreigners and domestic enemies. She reenacted a Resurrection scene every Friday that depicted her as the arisen. This play reinforced in her followers the belief in the Kongolese connection to the Divine Mother and the Crucified Savior. Both were cast as African/Black by Kimpa Vita. Kimpa Vita claimed that her biological son was immaculately conceived. She stated, "I cannot deny that he is mine, but how I had him, I do not know. I know, however, that he came to me fom heaven."

Kimpa Vita's approach brought her into conflict with Pedro IV who was among the most powerful claimants to the kingship in the Kongo. Pedro IV not only rejected Kimpa's spiritual/religious claims, but he was also under the influence of European priests that labeled Kimpa as a heretic. Vita increasingly became a thorn in the side of Pedro IV, as exemplified by her impatience with Pedro IV in reestablishing Sao Salvador and successfully resettling the capital herself. Kimpa was persuasive and appeared to be

Kongolese cross of the crucified Kimpa Vita. "Kongo Across The Waters" Exhibit as the New Orleans Museum of Art, 2015.

gaining momentum fast. Pedro IV's own wife converted to "Antonianism". Additionally, Pedro Constantinho da Silva Kibenga, who was a high-ranking commander of Pedro IV, also joined with Kimpa. Pedro IV was persuaded by Bernardo da Gallo and Lorenzo da Lucca, who were Catholic priests, to try and convict Kimpa Vita of heresy under "Kongo" law. In 1706 she was captured, convicted, and

18ᵗʰ century piece of Kimpa Vita presented as the Crucified Savior with her son on her hip. Also from the 2015 "Kongo Across The Water" exhibit at the New Orleans Museum of Art.

burned alive, along with her biological son. Her teachings remained influential in the region for many years after her death and many today still honor her as a matriarch of Angola.

It is fruitful to compare and contrast Kimpa Vita's experience to the great priestess Hypatia from Alexandria, Egypt, who was well known for her aptitude in various disciplines including math and science. In 415 CE Hypatia's death was fomented by church officials who had grown tired of being publically outwitted by Hypatia. Hypatia was branded a heretic. Like Kimpa Vita, Hypatia also had a large following. Her death was brutal, as was Kimpa Vita's. However, the misogyny that women faced, as Rome continuously dragged Europe into their Age of Darkness, differed from what Kimpa Vita would have faced in the early 1700's. The dedication to male supremacy survived, as did the notion that violence against non-adherents to Catholic doctrine was justified. However by the times of Kimpa Vita, a very strong racial component had emerged. Therefore Kimpa Vita fought to prevail against Africans and Europeans that perpetuated the misogynistic and racially bigoted practices of Europe, especially in the regions that they colonized.

Thus was the context in which the Black Madonna, and Black Jesus, began to worshipped only in private by church officials.

The Hidden Madonna

During the era of the Crusades, just like the Roman purge, it was common to hide texts, symbols, or statues that might result in harm being done to the owner. They also hid valuable texts so they would not be stolen, or destroyed by rivals. However, long after the Crusades, even in areas that were firmly under the control of Christians, we find the hiding and disappearance of Black Madonna statues. My personal experiences at the Houston museums aside, the reality of the hidden Madonnas is well-documented. One text that presents weighty evidence is *Anacalypsis: An Attempt to Draw Aside the Veil of the Saitic Isis*, which was published by Godfrey Higgins in 1833. Higgins proclaimed in Volume One his classic book *Anacalypsis* that:

> There is scarcely an old church in Italy where some remains of the worship of the BLACK VIRGIN and BLACK CHILD are not to be met with. Very often the black figures have given way to white ones, and in these cases the black ones, being held sacred, were put into retired paces in the churches, but were not destroyed, but are yet to be found there.[1]

Isn't it intriguing that the Black statues are not destroyed, but hidden and replaced with white ones?

This proclivity within the Catholic world to hide Black Madonnas is documented in detail in Ean Begg's *Cult of the Black Madonna*, which was initially published in 1985 and then revised in 1996. In his research, Begg revealed that the response from the church officials to inquiries regarding the Black Madonna most often ranged from dismissiveness to frustration. In *Cult of the Black Virgin* Begg documents a very telling experience of anthropologists Leonard W. Moss and Stephen C. Cappannari. At a gathering of the American Association for the Advancement of Science in December of

---

[1] Godfrey Higgins *Anacalypsis: An Attempt to Draw Asis the Veil of the Saitic Isis; or an Inquiry into the Origin of Languages, Nations and Religions, Volume One*, first published 1833. This edition was printed by University Books, Inc. (New York) in 1965. The quote is from pg. 138 of that text.

1952, every nun and priest in the room walked out when the two of them presented their research on the Black Madonna.[2]

Begg sought out to find specific Black Madonnas that are documented in historical writings. However many were either unheard of by local Catholic communities or the whereabouts of the statues were unknown. In 1945 Emile Salliens wrote in detail about a Black Madonna statue in the Ballon commune of France. She specified that it was made with earthenware, had been created about the 15th century, that it was in a private collection, and that a 19th century statue was in the adjacent parish. In regard to his visit there for his book that was published in 1985, Begg commented that, "None of the local inhabitants I spoke to could recall any particular Marian devotion".[3] A statue by the name of Our Lady of the Hollies at the French commune of Arfeuiles, France, who had been written about by three previous scholars as a Black Madonna, Salliens included, was no longer Black by the time of Begg's visit. Not only was there no remembrance of a Cult of the Black Virgin, but the statue had been taken away, repainted and returned as "refurbished". Such has been the fate of many well-aged Black Virgin statues - Black today, white tomorrow. Or even worse, Black today and gone tomorrow.

For the sake of humoring the reader, I will share here some of the absurd claims by adherents to the Catholic Church as to why the Virgin Mary statues are Black. The most common reason given is that the statues or paintings have

---

[2] Ean Begg, The Cult of the Black Virgin, (London: Penguin Books, 1985; revised 1996), pg. 8-9.
[3] Ibid, pg. 9.

become black by way of smoke damage or accumulation of dirt. On the surface of things this is quite laughable. The variance in color is clearly from paint. Church adherents have circled their wagons around the fallacy of the stoic, virgin, white Madonna. Another common claim is that the Black Madonna symbolizes mystery. This claim is short of the truth. She is shrouded in mystery however that is not quite her meaning. Throughout the Piscean Age the western world has succeeded in pulling the wool of the eyes of the multitudes. The Black Madonna is the divine mother that humans have worshipped for hundreds of thousands of years. She is the Mother of God; the primordial womb; she has the power to heal the sick; and repel enemies. As Asherah she was with El at the beginning of creation; as Auset, she revived Ausar and miraculously conceived Heru.

There is another reason that the Catholic Church would rather bypass meaningful discussion concerning the Black Madonna. If Virgin Mary, Mother of God is BLACK, then then that would necessarily mean that GOD is BLACK. By that that I mean that "Jesus", as he is cast in the Christian world as both flesh and God, is a Black man. This ultimately leads to the realization that the BLACK MAN is GOD. This reveals another ancient secret – that the Savior is a Black man. Let us recall Nat Turner, whose connection with the divine led him to organize the liberation of his own people, as a true Messiah would. Let us not forget Kimpa Vita, who was burned alive along with her seed/son. Every non-compliant Black man in the western world elicits fear that plays itself out in countless ways in western political, social, and legal constructs. The only hope of nullifying this threat of a Black Messiah, is to neutralize the Divine Mother of God. As we

nationalist activity, and interested in counterintelligence,
to coordinate this program. This Agent will be responsible
for the periodic progress letters being requested, but each
Agent working this type of case should participate in the
formulation of counterintelligence operations.

GOALS

For maximum effectiveness of the Counterintelligence
Program, and to prevent wasted effort, long-range goals are
being set.

1. Prevent the coalition of militant black
nationalist groups. In unity there is strength; a truism
that is no less valid for all its triteness. An effective
coalition of black nationalist groups might be the first
step toward a real "Mau Mau" in America, the beginning of
a true black revolution.

2. Prevent the rise of a "messiah" who could
unify, and electrify, the militant black nationalist movement.
Malcolm X might have been such a "messiah;" he is the martyr
of the movement today. Martin Luther King, Stokely Carmichael
and Elijah Muhammed all aspire to this position. Elijah
Muhammed is less of a threat because of his age. King could
be a very real contender for this position should he abandon
his supposed "obedience" to "white, liberal doctrines"
(nonviolence) and embrace black nationalism. Carmichael
has the necessary charisma to be a real threat in this way.

3. Prevent violence on the part of black
nationalist groups. This is of primary importance, and is,
of course, a goal of our investigative activity; it should
also be a goal of the Counterintelligence Program. Through
counterintelligence it should be possible to pinpoint potential
troublemakers and neutralize them before they exercise their
potential for violence.

4. Prevent militant black nationalist groups and
leaders from gaining respectability, by discrediting them
to three separate segments of the community. The goal of
discrediting black nationalists must be handled tactically
in three ways. You must discredit these groups and
individuals to, first, the responsible Negro community.
Second, they must be discredited to the white community,

- 3 -

In 1968 the FBI unleashed their extralegal COINTELPRO
against Black citizens. The second of the listed objectives
was to prevent the growth of a Black Messiah.

march closer and closer to the turning of time and the arrival of the Aquarius Age, the truths of human divinity and the Great Mother of all Ages will be revealed!

The Great Character Assassination

Popular culture also serves to divert the multitudes away for the true historical reality of who the Black Woman actually is. Popular culture reinforces social roles and social norms. This is repeatedly reflected in the world of entertainment. Popular culture reinforces a number of comforting stereotypes. These stereotypes are "caricatures of comfort" to the western psyche.

According to the research of Carolyn West, the roles by Black women in popular entertainment roughly fall into three stereotypical caricatures. The first stereotypical role is "Mammy", whose name comes from the faithful plantation servant in the 1939 movie "Gone With The Wind". Mammy's character, who is played by the actress Hattie McDaniel, is a loyal servant who cares for her owners with unwavering devotion. She may be a bit sassy, but it is understood that this sassiness is rooted in her love for her owners. We see the evolution of the "Mammy" framework in Esther Role's character as "Florida Evans" in the hit show *Good Times* and in Nell Carter's role as "Nell" in Gimme A Break. "Mammy" is typically fat, dark-skinned, and sassy. Ultimately she is the great caregiver to others. Furthermore, she is seldom sexual.

The second stereotypical character is "Sapphire". The name comes from the character "Sapphire Stevens" on the controversial 1950's show *Amos and Andy*. She was played by actress Ernistine Wade. "Sapphire" is often mean-spirited and manipulative. Unlike "Mammy" who is nurturing, "Sapphire" is outright confrontational. This stereotype is reflected in the characters of "Aunt Esther" that is played by LaWanda Page in the 1970s show Sanford and Son. Additionally, "Mary Lee Johnston", who was played by Mo'Nique in the film Previous was a rather sinister variation of "Sapphire". Thus "Sapphire" is a world wind. Another variation of "Sapphire" would be the "angry Black woman" stereotype or the belligerent Black female DMV worker for example.

The third caricature is "Jezebel". Jezebel is an ancient Caananite deity that eventually came to be presented in Christian doctrine as a woman that encouraged sexual immorality. The "Jezebel" stereotype played a major part through the years in justifying the sexual violence that was perpetrated against Black women and all women as a matter of fact throughout the Piscean Age. To the western psyche, all sexual violence against "Jezebel" was her fault, as she in some form or another welcomed or enjoyed the experience that was forced upon her. This is reflected in the depiction of model Grace Jones as sexual, animalistic, and in needed of taming. This motif is reflected both in her work as a model and an actress. Another is the "Olivia Pope" character in the TV series Scandal that debuted in 2012. Pope is played by actress Kerry Washington. Pope's character is most content as a lusty "sidechick". This fact is mitigated by the narrative that she is the sidechick of the president of the United States. Although Black senator Edison Davis, a seemingly upstanding Black man wants to be with her, her allegiance is to her the white, married president. There is no doubt that

"Angelfood McSpade" was a character in the Zap Comix comic book series that was published in the 1960's. Notice how Africa is denigrated in the image. Angelfood portrayed as unattractive and lustful. Her lips were large, her breasts and buttocks were oversized, and she was an ever-willing sexual object. She was repeatedly raped in the comic book including being forced to lick a toilet bowl while being forcefully penetrated. The willing Black victim of rape was born in the western psyche to justify their lust and rape. In order to reconcile their lust for supposed lesser humans, Europeans dehumanized their victims.

the scenario is a play on the western motif of the loyal, happy, Black "Jezebel". The "Jezebel" stereotype has served as the justification for countless physical and sexual violations through the years. Furthermore, this stereotype works against western fears of a living, awakened Black Madonna that seeks to bring forth the Crucified Savior.

Civilizations are living, breathing organisms with symptoms that indicate that change is necessary if western society is to survive. Although there are several "-isms" that require addressing, it appears to me that historical sexism has done nothing but to create a world of antagonism between the sexes. I surmise that a successful strategy to evolve past this issue would not only require change in the legislative realm, but would also require evolution in the realm of religion and spirituality. That evolution will be a revolution of sorts because it will require the return of the divine Black Mother of God to her rightful place.

The "Mammy" Stereotype

Hattie McDaniel as "Mammy" in the 1939 film *Gone With The Wind.*

Esther Rolle as "Florida Evans" in the 1970's TV show *Good Times*.

The "Sapphire" Stereotype

LaWanda Page as the character "Esther" in the TV sitcom *Sanford and Son*.

Mo'Nique as "Mary Lee Johnston" in the 2009 film *Precious*.

The "Jezebel" Stereotype

Model and actress Grace Jones pictured in a cage with a small sign reading "DO NOT FEED THE ANIMAL".

Kerrie Washington as "Olivia Pope" in the TV series *Scandal*.

Positive representation is necessary to eradicate the psychological and cultural damage that was done throughout the Piscean Age.

"Michelle Obama" is a 2018 portrait of Michelle Obama by the artist Amy Sherald for the National Portrait Gallery.

Oshun, river goddess of Ifa spirituality.

Danai Gurira as Okoye in *Black Panther*.

Made in the USA
Las Vegas, NV
22 January 2023

66052286R00050